Owoseni Adebowale

Application of Soft Systems Methodology (SSM) in a Swedish State University Resource Allocation Problem

GRIN Publishing

Bibliographic information published by the German National Library:

The German National Library lists this publication in the National Bibliography; detailed bibliographic data are available on the Internet at http://dnb.dnb.de .

Imprint:

Copyright © 2010 GRIN Verlag GmbH
Print and binding: Books on Demand GmbH, Norderstedt Germany
ISBN: 978-3-640-81172-4

This book at GRIN:

http://www.grin.com/en/e-book/165454/application-of-soft-systems-methodology-ssm-in-a-swedish-state-university

GRIN - Your knowledge has value

Since its foundation in 1998, GRIN has specialized in publishing academic texts by students, college teachers and other academics as e-book and printed book. The website www.grin.com is an ideal platform for presenting term papers, final papers, scientific essays, dissertations and specialist books.

Visit us on the internet:

http://www.grin.com/

http://www.facebook.com/grincom

http://www.twitter.com/grin_com

Blekinge Institute of Technology

Master in Informatics

Fundamental Information System Issues

Moment 3

General Systems Theory

Application of Soft Systems Methodology (SSM) in a Swedish State University Resource Allocation Problem

By

Adebowale Oluropo Owoseni

Germaine Joy Imhanyehor

Zilethilwe Zuleikyah Steinbach

November 2010

Application of Soft Systems Methodology (SSM) in a Swedish State University Resource Allocation Problem

Zilethilwe Z. Steinbach, Germaine J. Imhanyehor, Adebowale O. Owoseni

Informatics Department
Blekinge Institute of Technology
Karlskrona, Sweden

Abstract

Funding and resource allocation in a Swedish university is fast degenerating to a problematic situation. This write-up applied soft system methodology to the situation, it placed the 'problems' in perspective and came up with a conceptual model of the problematic situation. A conclusion was drawn by comparing the model with the actual problem description.

1.0 Introduction

Soft System Methodology (SSM) as introduced by Checkland's in the 1970s is not a direct problem solving concept, it simply provide a way of re-illustrating a problematic situation. SSM derived its strength from one of the system myths that says *"The best thing that can be done to a problem is to dissolve it, to redesign the entity to eliminate the problem"* [2]. SSM helps in creating radically different perspective of the problematic area; it redefines the system in such a way that the problem is no longer a problem [3]

We adopt a six step approach in applying SSM to the problematic situation,

1. Describe problematic Situation
2. Draw a rich picture showing all components of the system and information, money and material flows
3. Define subsystems
4. Create root definitions
5. Create conceptual models
6. Compare model with actual problem definition

The description of the problematic situation we are considering in this write-up is available in the assignment text [3]; it hovers around resource allocation in a Swedish state university.

Next is the rich picture diagram.

2.0 The Rich Picture

Considering the peculiarities of the team work vis-à-vis our geographic location and timing, the best option we had was to arrange a virtual discussion session on Skype. We use a screen sharing and video conferencing tools available in Skype. In our virtual discussion session, we identified the system border, suggested all possible components within and outside the system border, this components have direct or indirect relationship with the description of the problematic situation. After identifying the components we looked at the relationship within the components of the system in terms of information, material and money flow. We all drew individual draft diagrams of the rich picture on plane sheet of paper. One of the pictures is shown in figure 2.0a

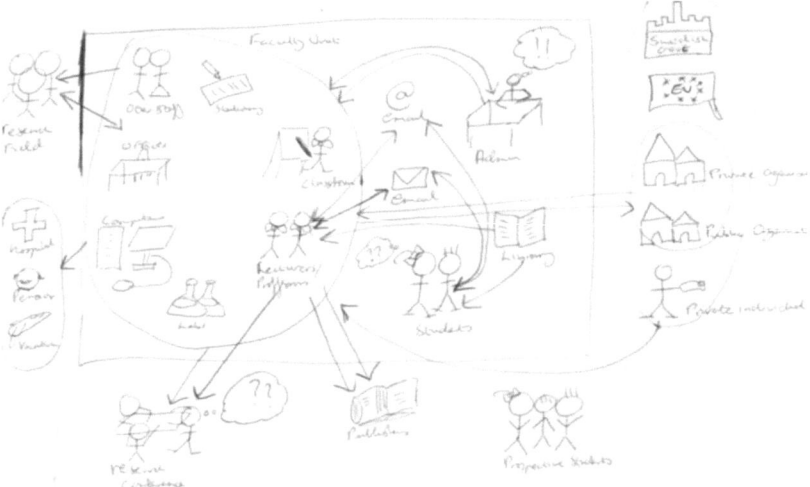

Figure 2.0a: Raw Rich Picture (Initial Manual Draft)

The raw diagram was transformed with *Microsoft Visio*, figure 2.0b shows the defined system and all identified components

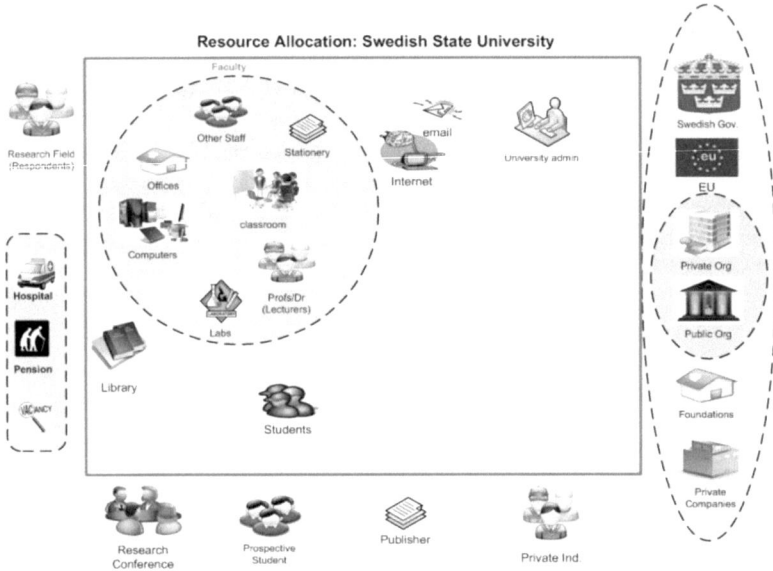

Figure 2.0b: Rich Picture – Defined boundary and system components

The Swedish state university is the system boundary, outside the boundary, we identified the following components:

- **Founding Partners**: These include Swedish Government, European Union, private organizations, public organizations, foundations, private companies and private individuals
- **Research Fields**: These represent location where researchers retrieved raw data. In case of social research, the research field could be a target group of people or respondents to some sorts of questionnaires or interviews. It could also represent locations where experiment materials are obtained for scientific laboratories research.
- **Research Conference**: Gathering of researchers to share idea
- **Prospective Student:** Incoming students that may be indirectly affected by funding policies of the university
- **Publishers of research papers**: these include all publishers of research papers, it may include in-house university publishers but they will not been seen as local to the university since they publish papers from other researchers outside the university.

- **Providers of Social Support Services:** these include the hospitals, pension, vacancy adverts, and other social benefits sponsored by the university.

Inside the boundary we have the following:

- **University Admin**: Oversees the faculties and liaise with funding bodies.
- **Internet**: We looked at internet as compound component with sub-components like email, e-learning platforms, websites etc. we decided not to dwell on these subcomponents because it plays a passive role in the bigger picture of the *funding* system; we could have consider the details if we are target system is *"Learning in Swedish state university"*.
- **Professors / Researchers /Teachers**: This component includes all individuals responsible for teaching; it could be research or academic teaching. It also refer to researchers that are teachers at the same time.
- **Students /PHD Students:** Research student or academic student
- **Other staff:** These include all Non- academic staffs of the faculty like laboratory attendants, library attendants, research assistants etc
- Others include **Stationeries, Laboratories, Computers, Classrooms** and *offices*

The next step was the flows; as shown in figure 2.0b

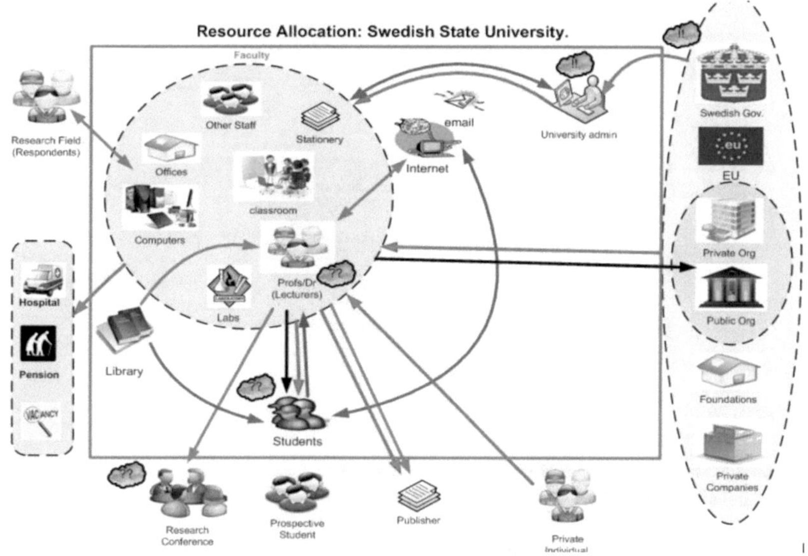

Figure 2.0c: Rich Picture – Information, Material and Monetary Flow

Red, green and black arrows shows money, Information and '*Knowledge*', flow respectively; the knowledge flow is seen as a special type of information flow –"*Teaching*" provided by the faculty (teachers) to the students and private/public organizations. The blue clouds represent some confusion that may exist in the following areas

- Researcher's research result, and the opinion of other researchers in research conference
- The students / teacher learning expectations
- University Administrators and Funding organizations confusions concerning how to make good use of the monetary allocation or resources available to the university

The next step was to identify potential or real conflict in the diagram as shown in figure 2.0d

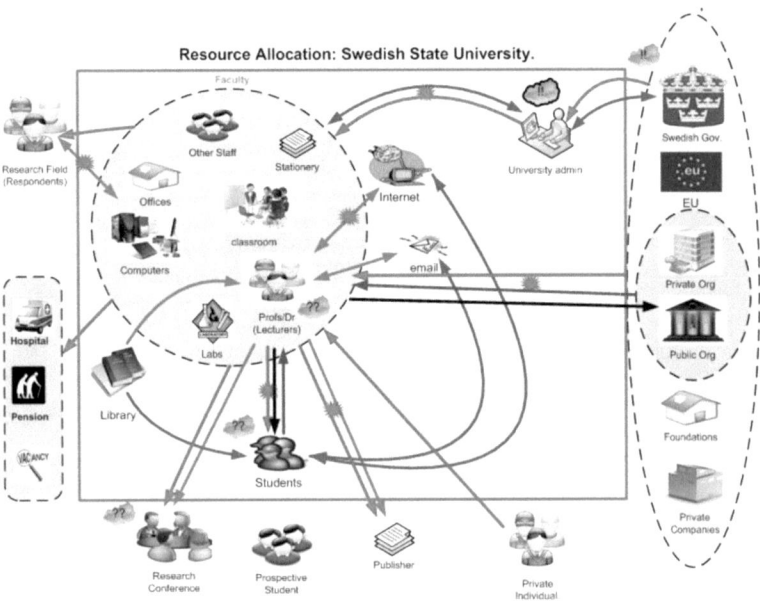

Figure 2.0d: Rich Picture – Information, Material and Monetary Flow

A number of potential or real conflict areas were identified, the red splash is used to identify these areas; they include:

- **Faculty and University Administrator:** How to effectively allocate available money to all cost centers like teaching, research, development etc.

- **Researcher and Publisher**: Which publisher should the researcher sent the research paper to? What the criteria are for publish a paper?
- **Research Field and Researcher**: Where to get raw data, the problem of getting accurate data in social research; are the respondent sincere?
- **Funding**: The decision of who to fund?
- **Internet**: Bandwidth problem and system availability
- **Teaching**: Conflict between what to do per time, researching or teaching?

The next step is identification of sub-systems.

3.0 Defining Subsystems

The basic criterion for selecting subsystems is the strong internal interaction within related components. We identified ten subsystems as shown in figures 3.0a, 3.0b and 3.0c.

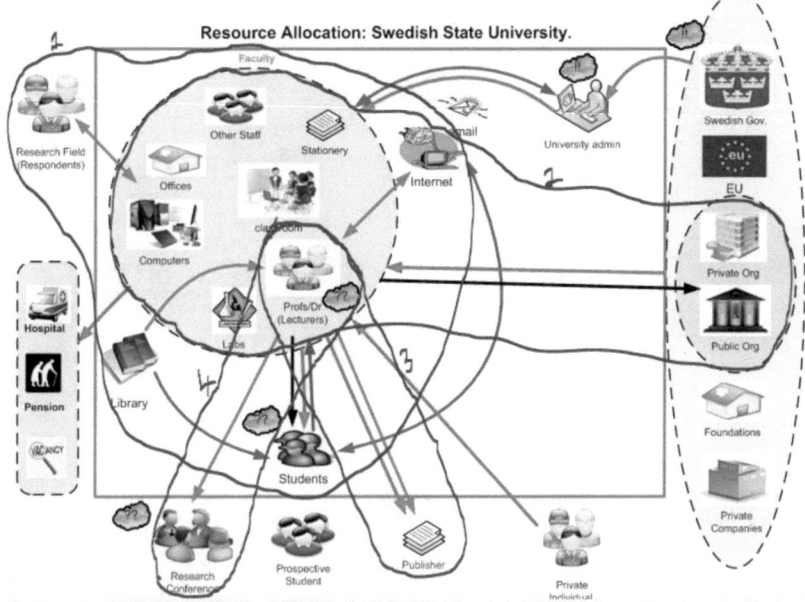

Figure 3.0a: Rich Picture – showing subsystems 1 - 4

Subsystem 1- Research Supervision: This handles the process of impacting the *act and science of researching* into research students

Subsystem 2 - *Professional Teaching:* This system deals with knowledge transfer between the university and to professionals (employees) of private/public organizations. The transfer could be achieved through lectures, seminars or short courses.

Subsystem 3- *Research Publishing:* This subsystem makes research outcome available to the public in an organized manner; a way that will protect the right of the researcher and generate income for publisher.

Subsystem 4 - *Research Conferencing*: This deals with the process of knowledge sharing within community of researchers

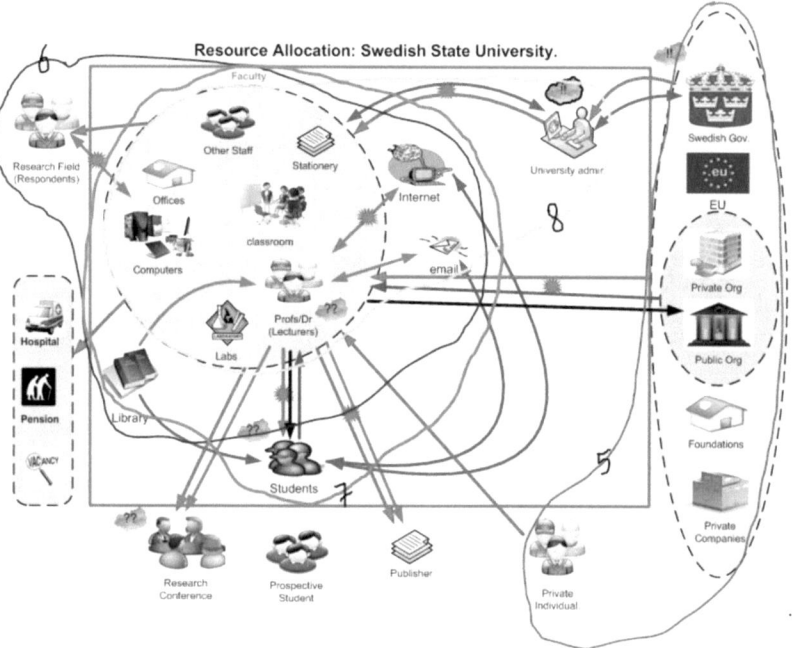

Figure 3.0b: Rich Picture – showing subsystems 5 - 8

Subsystem 5 - *University Funding:* The subsystem looks at how money is allocated to the university and how the money is being utilized.

Subsystem 6 - *Research data collection and processing Activity:* The purpose of the system is to acquire meaningless data, process it and come up with scientific facts and principles.

Subsystem 7 - *Academic Teaching:* Here, Students acquire knowledge through academic study activities.

Subsystem 8 - Faculty Administration: This looks at how the faculty resources are being utilized in line with The EU standards in order to avoid conflicts.

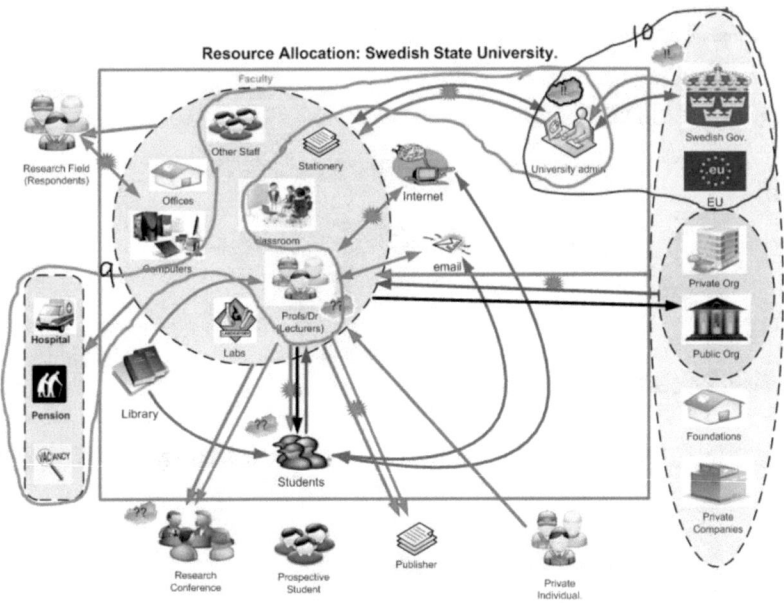

Figure 3.0c: Rich Picture – showing subsystems 9 and 10

Subsystem 9 - Staff Social Welfare: This subsystem simply ensures the welfare of staff

Subsystem 10 - University Resource Control: This deals with how government funds is managed by the university

4.0 Creating Root Definitions

We create root definitions (RD) for subsystems identified in previous section. We used a template similar to the one used in SSM sample of Msc. Informatics Problematic Situation [2]. The template describes each RD in understandable details.

Name of Subsystem	1: Research Supervision Subsystem
Client	Students (PhD students mainly)
Actor	Teachers / Professors
Transformation	Research rudiments (knowledge) are transferred from researchers to students
Weltanschauung	Students carry out research activities based on supervision and guidelines they received from their Teachers
Owner	Faculty
Environment	Research field, Classroom, laboratory
Discussion	The sub system is an knowledge transfer system where the art and science of 'Research' is acquired.
Final RD	The students should be supervised when conducting research.

Name of Subsystem	2: Professional Teaching Subsystem
Client	Professional in Private/Public Organizations
Actor	Professors /Lecturers
Transformation	Knowledge in form of lectures/seminars relayed(transferred) to employees of private/public organizations
Weltanschauung	The employees of private/public organizations are eager to learn
Owner	Professors /Lecturers
Environment	Internet, classroom
Discussion	This subsystem is seen as a system for information and knowledge transfer, from teachers to the employees of public/private organizations.
Final RD	Provide courses that interest private and public organizations at a fee

Name of Subsystem	3: Research Publishing subsystem
Client	Professor (Researcher)
Actor	Publisher
Transformation	Receive research outcomes from researchers, publish in a reference - able platform (eBooks or magazines)
Weltanschauung	The final research outcome inform of scientific papers are published and printed by a publisher
Owner	Publisher
Environment	Scientific Journal
Discussion	The subsystem simply make research outcome available to the public in an organized manner that will protect the right of the researcher and generate income for publisher.

Final RD	The researcher makes research outcome inform of scientific paper available to publisher for publishing to general public in an organized manner

Name of Subsystem	4:Research Conferencing system
Client	Research Conference
Actor	Professors
Transformation	Researcher provide presents outcome of research activity, the authenticity of outcome is argued among professional in research field, knowledge is shared and new research opportunities revealed
Weltanschauung	Research outcomes are shared and knowledge transferred between researchers
Owner	Researchers (Professors)
Environment	Research conferences, symposiums
Discussion	The subsystem basically is an avenue to share research experience and outcome
Final RD	Research outcome should be shared among researchers in order to gain knowledge and expose new research opportunities

Name of Subsystem	5: University funding subsystem
Client	Students, Researchers, Teachers, other staff
Actor	Swedish Government, European Union, private individuals, private/public organizations
Transformation	Money is give to University and researchers in form of grants and funds. University in turn provide research and academic teaching to students, while researchers spend money on research activities
Weltanschauung	Money is made available to the university and researchers for the purpose of administration, teaching and researching
Owner	Swedish Government
Environment	University Administration
Discussion	The subsystem looks at how money is allocated to the university and how the money is being spent
Final RD	Swedish Government, European Union, private individuals, private/public organizations provide money to the university and expects good stewardship and accountability after a given period, statement of spending will determine subsequent funds allocation to the university.

Name of Subsystem	6: Research data collection and processing subsystem
Client	Research field
Actor	Researchers (Professor/PhD students)
Transformation	Research groups conduct research and information from research get published as papers
Weltanschauung	Establish scientific theories based on facts obtained from research data collection and processing.
Owner	Researchers (Professor/PhD students)
Environment	Laboratory
Discussion	The purpose of the system is to acquire meaningless data, process it and come up with scientific facts and principles
Final RD	Collect Raw data , processed with scientific methods, obtain results, analyze results and establish novel facts

Name of Subsystem	7: Academic Teaching subsystem
Client	Students
Actor	Teachers
Transformation	Teacher exchange information with students so that students are more informed and knowledgeable
Weltanschauung	Knowledge is impacted into students through the process of teaching
Owner	Teacher
Environment	Classroom, library
Discussion	Students acquire knowledge through academic study activities
Final RD	Teachers should teach students, they should exchange information required to build desired knowledge in students

Name of Subsystem	8: Faculty Administration Subsystem
Client	Teachers, Researchers, Other staff, students
Actor	University Administrator
Transformation	Faculty provide enabling teaching and research environment and in turn receives academic and research activity reports
Weltanschauung	Costs incurred from the research group must be recovered from faculty resource
Owner	Teachers, Researchers, Other staff,
Environment	Faculty Administrative tools
Discussion	Faculty administration should be careful enough not to allow teaching and research funds to mix up. The EU standard should be protected in order to avoid conflicts.
Final RD	Funds provided for research should not mix with funds provided for teaching.

Name of Subsystem	9: Staff Social Welfare Subsystem
Client	Researchers, Teachers, Professors, Other staff
Actor	Hospital, Pension fund, Vacation fund
Transformation	The Faculty/ University provide funds and the 'Actors' in turn provide corresponding services
Weltanschauung	The staff pays a percentage of their salaries to enjoy the benefits in the future. The staff should be willing to pay.
Owner	Researchers, Teachers, Professors, Other staff
Environment	Social security scheme
Discussion	The subsystem ensures the welfare of staff
Final RD	Money deducted from the teachers and staff added with government provision helps with pension ,medical and vacation benefits in the future

Name of Subsystem	10: University Resource Control Subsystem
Client	University Administrator
Actor	University Administrator, Swedish Government, European Union
Transformation	Funds is provided by Government, reports of how fund is managed is made available to the government by the University admin
Weltanschauung	Promoting transparent and prudent funds management
Owner	Swedish Government, European Union
Environment	Financial Report
Discussion	Deals with how government funds is managed by the university
Final RD	Swedish Government and EU provide funds to university and the university in turn provides yearly financial report.

Having obtained root definitions for each subsystems identified in the rich diagram, we then combine all the RDs together in form of a story. Here is the first trial:

The students should be supervised when conducting research. Provide courses that interest private and public organizations at a fee. The researcher makes research outcome inform of scientific paper available to publisher for publishing to general public in an organized manner. Swedish Government, European Union, private individuals, private/public organizations provide money to the university and expect good stewardship and accountability after a given period, statement of spending will determine subsequent funds allocation to the university. Collect raw data, processed with scientific methods, obtain results, analyze results and establish novel facts. Teachers should teach students, they should exchange information required to build desired knowledge in students. Funds provided for research should not mix with funds provided for teaching. Money deducted from the teachers and staff added with government provision helps with pension, medical and vacation benefits in the future. Swedish Government and EU provide funds to university and the university in turn provides yearly financial report.

The sentences were edited and rearranged in order to make the story logical and understandable; here is the edited version of RD story:

Teachers should teach and impact desired knowledge into students, ideally students should be supervised when conducting research. Researchers collect raw data, processed it with scientific methods, obtain results, analyze results and establish novel facts. They present research outcomes in scientific papers; they make it available to publisher for publishing to general public in an organized manner. Money provided for research should not be mixed up with money provided for teaching. Money deducted from teachers' and other staff salaries, with government provisions, helps with medical, pension and vacation benefits. The Faculty should provide courses of interest to private and public organizations at a fee. Swedish Government, European Union, private individuals, private and public organizations provide money into the university and expect good stewardship and accountability. The university provides yearly financial report to EU and Swedish government which shall determine subsequent funds allocation for the next academic year.

Having derived a logical and understandable RD story, the next step is to conceptualize the new problem situation perspective as presented in the story

5.0 Conceptual Model

The conceptual model is simply a graphical representation of the new problem perspective derived from the root definition story. The first step in drawing the model is to identify all verbs in the RD story, the verbs represents some form of activities. For each of the verbs there is at least one associated noun or pronoun (subject or object in vocabulary) which indicates who is performing an activity or who the recipient of an activity is. We also look at details of each identified activity to ascertain how, when and what is done. These details are represented in the conceptual model as shown in Figure 5.0a.

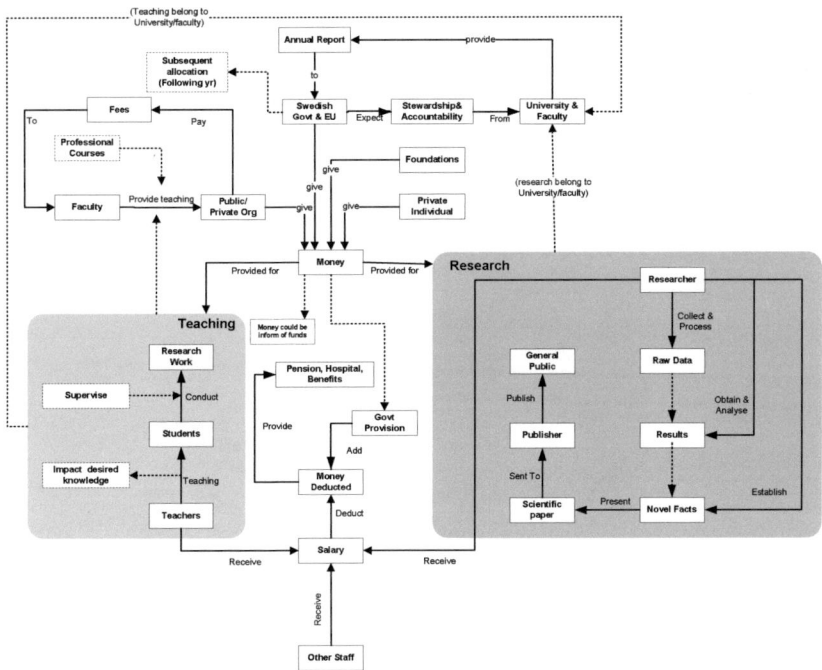

Figure 5.0a Conceptual Model.

6.0 Conclusion

Comparing the problem situation with the final conceptual model, a number of similarities can be identified, but the conceptualized problem looks quite simple and approachable. The outcome of this exercise has buttressed the fact that Soft Systems Methodology is not a problem solving paradigm, it only re-present a problematic situation in a lighter, less ambiguous and understandable form.

References

[1] Per Flensbuge. An Example using SSM retrieved on 10th Nov. 2010 from http://informaticsnetwork.se/SSM/Index.html

[2] BIBLIOGRAPHY Russell Ackoff. Myths about systems retrieved on 10th Nov. 2010from http://ikt.ei.hv.se/personal/impf/per/Master/Ackoffmyths.ppt

[3] Sytem Theory - Moment 3 Guide. retrieved on 10th Nov 2010 from https://bth.itslearning.com/file/download.aspx?FileID=506233&FileVersionID=-1.

[4] Tom Gross (2008) *Soft System Methodology*. Retrieved on 8th Nov. 2010 from http://en.wikipedia.org/wiki/Soft_systems_methodology

[5] C. E. Shannon, "A mathematical theory of communication," Bell System Technical Journal, vol. 27, pp. 379-423 and 623-656, July and October, 1948 – A classical text about communication